T0128463

Silent Music

Volume 1

ANTHONY LEWIS

authorHOUSE®

AuthorHouse™
1663 Liberty Drive
Bloomington, IN 47403
www.authorhouse.com
Phone: 833-262-8899

Published by AuthorHouse 03/29/2023

ISBN: 979-8-8230-0476-3 (sc)
ISBN: 979-8-8230-0474-9 (hc)
ISBN: 979-8-8230-0475-6 (e)

Library of Congress Control Number: 2023905856

Print information available on the last page.

Anticipating the pain with ever step

It's The pressure underneath
Sore ceiling as they sag
A trace with every step
The troubles are in the arch
Down, set, Let's start, Take another step
He keeps moving, even though some things fall apart
If he could have seen the future, he would have brace for this part
Splat!!!," Damn, I wish I would have know about this part
Pushing off the ground, getting back up, Balancing, That's the hard part
Swinging, "Get Away!!!"
"Boy I tell you, You got heart
With age one is brittle, soft and sweet like a skittle
Bands sing songs like fiddles
The pain starts when it goes towards the middle
The persistence of remarkable people

#2

fiddle or fally

Was he mistaken or was he a fraud
Nose snarling, "On God."
They got along together like two peas in a pod
What made you do it Todd?
"I was doing it for my job."
"You know, I thought if I didn't do it"
"I'd get fired."
Chuckling, Awaiting a handshake
"Well your hired
"I don't know what you had to do to get hired"
"He didn't do what he was supposed to do
And He got fired"
"He got fired"
"Yea he got fired"
"And now you got hired."

#3

Ton tow

In Toronto in a bronco
Rolling in the snow
I'm in another city
I had to let her go
She wasn't faithful
She was fucking with olds man's bro
It hurt for a little bit
Then I had to let it go
A few tears drops
Enough to make it flow
I was hurt, I didn't know where to go
Seen a picture on a social media site
I was like that's where I'mma go
I guess thats the place where i needed to go
It's so cold, I ain't worried about that no mo

#4

who cares is she's a whore
"here you go, maim
opening the door up
People like that make me sick and wanna throw up
Hold on, "let me back up"
I was late let me ketchup and packet
Its perfect and clean
It's immaculate
It's so pretty, look at that
Hold on girl, let me take a picture
An unknown number calls, stops the picture
It's the Small things you capture
If your in love, you better chase after
Because when it's gone it'll be one thing sought after
Looking at the photos recreating the laughter
Embracing Love like the hug, when you say I love you after

#5

I get it
something is bothering you and
Making you upset
I can tell you and
Show you
That everything and
Everyone will be alright
Lost in his mind
He feels certain things are right
That's life of the black and white
The pages that you flip through every night
Hard to see with a blurry sight
Adjusting glasses, so it can be seen
Yeap, I think that's what it means
Hey baby can you check on that pot mustard green
I'm starting to see what mad Oscar grouch so mean

One day your gonna have to grow up
Clean and pick them up
Drops them off
Tellem we're here
Now it's time to get out
Wipe those tears
Blow it off
dust it off
Life is about falling
Getting back up
Brushing it off
Excuse me
that was an accident
I was just testing an experiment
With the results of resiliency
Come on give everyone and hand

#7

And see that it's you
Coconut brown skin
Coconut meat white in your eyes
Can you see the coconut brown in your eyes
Your the coconut that fell from the sky
Clonked me on my head
Now I can't keep you out of my head
I remember when I kid eyes on you
And then boom
I got hit by you
Out of the blurr I'm sitting next you
Was it god who dropped it out the sky
On the pews sitting next you
Good words from the lord
That's what where gonna do
I knew you where the one when I met you

#8

Your blaming everyone except you
No one is even doing anything to you
Just people really being genuine to you
Is there a reason to be really to be mean you
You know what I mean
No I don't
That's why I'm asking questions
How can we solve the problem without answering the questions
Hold on, she has an opinion
Aht, you know I had to step in
You think it's funny with that grin
No I don't think it was funny
It just reminded me that one theme I was in love
He was sweet he came over and drained the plug
Thank you so much
The key is under the rug

#9

No one is even around you and your
blaming someone else.
frustrated looking for some one to blame
Hey man I think you need to bowl in your lane
How about you mind your business man
I was until he stepped in
It's gonna be an Even fight around here
Nobody gets jumped round here
You got a problem
You identify the issues
What is it these time
She don't miss you
I get it
here's the tissue
Sniffling don't worry she's coming to get you.
Do you remember when y'all use to hug and kiss
Say I'm sorry and I forgive you

#10

Your standing right there saying b…..
Bye I don't want to her this
Well you should have thought about it
Sitting back and listening to arguments
Looking out the window, I didn't want it to come out like this
Let me calm down before I kill this b….
I see something is frustrating
I'll leave it there for the fixing
Stop it I don't want you to fix it
Then why is you bring it up
Sometimes I talk to myself
Don't mind me I'm just venting
You don't need to do anything
I just want to sort out some things
Oh excuse me did you want to say something
Off topic, yeah girl you're queen

#11

But I don't want to hear this
This was something He wanted to dodge
They threw n missed
Taunting, you can't hit
Smack he got hit
Day dreaming in class flick
The teacher is waiting on her answer
Come on !!, now you got this
Knuckle head Dimwit
Bulging more than a basketball with a tit
Your the one I'm in love with
I was wondering if I could give you kiss
I'll get in trouble to stay after the other kids get dismissed
Being here with you is lovely I don't mind being in detention
It seems like this is only way to get your undivided attention
I ll be thinking about you even if they give me a suspension

#12

The more you hold someone back
You increase the tension
Propellers on airplane
On a launchpad
Propelled like a bearing in a slingshot
Flup!! They nailed the bullseye the center dot
Oddly off on another plot
The climax is the spot
Overcoming obstacles
They seen it coming audibles
They fell for it
Down set hut
Egyptians queens and kings
Attention
Love was just enough
When the world cost so much

#13

Heavenly Father
I come to you
If I go to them why bother
It bothers me that I'm not the starting
I know I'm the one who should be playing
I hear what your saying
Sometimes when your not playing
Your winning
You'll be called into action
To come back for the winning
In a deficit
Can you help us out of predicament
We'll see
Victory !!! Is how it went
He put you in when it was time to represent
Just be ready on the side line or waiting bench

#14

I'll be your moon in your darkest hour
I'll be the knight that rescues you from the tallest tower
I'll be your sugar when your drink is sour
I'll be your energy when you need power

I'll be the fragrance of your flower
I'll be the seconds and the minutes of your hour
I'll be your substance that you need to devour
I'll stay with you until your last hour

I'll be your love when you need a shower
I'll be your change when you need a dollar
I'll be your voice wha as en you need to holler
I'll be the charm on your collar
I'll be your number one follower
I'll be your courage when you fell like a coward
I'll sit with you in the loneliest hour
I'll be your encouragement when you need to be empowered

#15

Country evenings and cool temperatures
I nice moment to be cuddle up
Looking at the stars pointing up
Shooting stars fall at angle to the left
The wind blows the chills felt in the elbows and chest
Sleepy eyes why don't we give a rest
Waking up, last night I thought we where gonna have sex
If I would known I would have shown up and did my best
I can't read your mind
You where sleeping
You feel asleep on my chest
Can you hear my heart beat
I can feel your heart beat on my chest
I'm getting sleepy eyed to
I think I need my rest
The choice I made, maybe one of the best

#16

I love you
Why did you have to say like that
The man behind the I love you
I was just saying it back
Don't turn into something that it's not
I meant what I said
I wasn't sarcastically saying it back
I'm compelled to tell you it back
I really do feel like that
Soon as I touch you
I want to rub you back
This tension in your back
Is that the spot where they stabbed you in the back
Smooth strokes to decompress the stress from way back
Don't worry about carry that
You got a new bag, no need for that

#17

I stay out the way
So they can't find a nigga to lock away
My boy didn't do nothing but he got locked away
Court and lawyers are out the way
One's are suppose to fight for you while your away
He showed up and fought all the way
She backed and walked away
The judge was like alright and okay
Sitting on the bench god moved somethings out off the way
Meditation and attractions blessings hurled down this way
Jehovah or Yahwey
Prayers In the morning,
afternoon and nightly sessions
Finally some rest and
Peace of mind and
Lord continue to hold my hand

On a corner with a beer
Talking about the next move
I love the spot I'm in
She wants to move
We gotta change the spot we kicking in
Moving up and up again
Looking at the spots I used to stay in
I know better is coming
I knew I wanted a bigger space
Now look at the space
If I go outside I can see outer space
Confined to a small space
Prayers, one day I'mma make it out this place
I had dreams I'm was the only person in that place
Going in circles
It's just me in that space

#19

Life is so beautiful
But your messing it up
With all that Arguing and fighting
Who cares who's gets the last words in
Your messing up the groove for tonight and
Time out what's really the reason for the bickering
It's so funny he's snickering
Everything is so funny mimicking
The thoughts while steering
Cruising I gotta make it to this spot
I chill place from all the hots spots
Are you online
No I'm not
I'm next to you in your spot
It seems like the tension came home from the other spot
Let me roll over in my spot

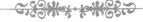

#20

I'm falling I'm wondering whose going to catch me
I'm hoping it's you
Thank you for what you do
You really got a lot of potential
Don't you know your real influential
I know your gonna hold down
I can see the stent in you
No band -aid toilet tissue
My heart pumps in four chambers
Just for you
In secret spot with you
That's a fifth for you
You sneezed that's a bless you
Awww chuh, don't mess with me fool
I'm so cold I don't wanna give it to you
I love you so much this song is for you

#21

Selfie in the restroom
On the wall they better make room
Don't you see a nigga in the room
A nigga so manly he made her jump the broom
She use to be behind the desk
Bellhop
Now it's family time at breakfast ihop
The love I have for you won't stop
Cupid help me
Pop !!!with one shot
Lovers ask me all the time
how did you get the panties to drop
I guess she got hot
She already told me I couldn't be in that that spot
Clearly she made it clear, sure why not
That's the reason I'm in the restroom with you at this spot

#22

I only want you
These other women that they you come up with
that's only in their imagination and you
I see you
But this time the only person you can blame is you
I can't take the blame for you
I can't do the time for you
I'll do the time for me
You do the time for you
When this is all over
I'll be glad to see you
It's been awhile
I've been waiting on you
Daddy loves you
Forget what the other people told you
I'll be here waiting you

#23

What does a father do
Sometimes I really can't talk to you
Because your not a father
But I'm listening to what your saying what you would do
If I was a father this is what I what do
Eureka that's what my father would have to do
He did it
Don't fathers know what to do
Sitting in silence praying for you
You can see them going down the wrong path
And the responsibility is on you
It's out of control
What was he supposed to do
Anything said can be used against you
He just said something to help you
Tables turned around it had nothing to do with you

#24

Tear drops fall
I love it when you call
I don't care when you stop by
It can be the summer winter or the fall
Just like leaves fall
I love expecting your call
So when is the next time your gonn call
Y'all shut up it's that call
Oh my god, I know y'all
I'm excited to see you and tellem I'm happy for y'all
Congratulations plaques on the wall
Pictures of you
I love seeing y'all
I know he's on a court somewhere playing ball
No need to be sad with y'all
Just waiting for my time writing letter to y'all

#25

Locked up
it ain't nothing like hearing your voice when I get chance to make call
Besides daddy and you
I don't know who to call
Ring ring ring
I didn't know if you'd accept the charges
We know it bullshit
If you fight bull shit with bullshit
It's just two chiefs chunking shit
We all know they only did it for the money
They ain't got no money
False charges to get paid
Taking our money
So all they want is our money
So they'll have money
After paying all the charges I don't have no money

#26

Huhhhgh
Sipping rosea for the day
Hanging with big boss
I gotta little Rickey Roseau in me
On theses freeways
On this information highway
I hope they hear me
I dodge them when they try to smear queer
Killa man is how we play it down here
From Texas to Florida they hear us down here
The south got something say
All that hating is blocking your way
I ain't gotta shoulder lean or rock away
I just walked away
One day it's gone be my day
I can feel it today was my day

#27

I'm spinning up
While there praying Jesus
Yes lord
Thank lord
I'm going to the next level
I'm spinning up
Blue ball
I'm sonic the hedge hog
Ching!!! I got hit like y'all
When there done praying
I can play y'all
A stinging pinch
Caused me to get hit
After charging up my ball
Shaking and yelling yes lawd
I bet that level yes lawd

#28

I'm surprised she called
Looking over his shoulder she sees who calls
Later own
Who was that called
Your already know who that was when they called
Are you hiding something because you get suspicious on the phone
I knew it was something getting of the phone
Matter fact why are your asking me all of the questions on the phone
Do I ask you who your talking to on the phone
That was unbelievable
How could you come up this
It was all on my own
Silently sitting at home
I can hear my thought rattling in my dome
Attention!!! A kavlar is on my dome
I fought for the USA this is my home

#29

life flight
He's loaded up
He got injured
He got blown up
Fire
pressure
Clothes got torn up
A new identity
I'm Jason Borned up
Airborne
In the sky
Wheels up
Airborne Soldiers
Attention
Right face
Loaded it up

#30

1500 or nothing
You niggas tripping
Hanging with nispey
A nigga learning from a g
Sergeants in the street
Generals at they desk
Dragging they feet
Telling a nigga how to move in the streets
That's sounds cool but that not how they move in the street
Different blocks different spots
If you don't know nobody you could shot
Ain't no safe place you could be at home and get shot
Niggas be at home wondering why they in the same spot
The wind is blowing they can set sail and get out
Ships pulling out the dock
Hope they don't get done like Jack, I'll never let go, and watch him drop

#31

This hit goes out to the bosses
Challenging them to one on one combat when they get off
I didn't even spit anything and the mic got dropped
Gottem stuck in one spot
looking like a head got cut off
Look at it roll around
His head got popped off
I told you I was gone do it I told you about popping off
Leveling up ain't no getting off
I had no other choice but to do it while I was off
That last time we had garbage I took it out when It was time to get off
Don't miss abuse it
Properly use it
Do you need it
No let's weed it
Unwrapped we really needed this

#32

A nigga kinda mischievous
I wonder why these niggas envious
We're just being us
I didn't mean to cuss
A showboat about that and with a wink yeah that's us
About that we won't fuss
We'll party in the club
We'll party on the bus
I don't know why they're fucking with us
We bought our own bottle at the club
They're looking up
Off course we gotta look down
Yeah you can come up and get down
Big baller for the night
I love when we get down
Hey hey it's Time for y'all to get down

#33

I'm at the bar drinking
And this song came on
An it had me thinking
Wondering why they say
I do too much drinking
I don't think so
I do it to drown out the overthinking
I can't tell you what's he's thinking
I know the reason why I'm drinking
Puzzled it got him really thinking
I'm astonished on how much you been drinking
We'll hell this ain't nothing
This is a light night
Insomniac drinking to drown out the overthinking thoughts at night
Woo-ooh it's a spooky night
Nawh kid we were just intrusions thoughts fucking with you for the night

#34

Keep it popping
Keep moving forward
Like a frog keep it hopping
Watch out for the apples that be dropping
Even bigger worries watch out for the coconuts that be dropping
Cazy coco loco she done called the po pos
Answering questions, oh no!!!
Lies !!!we already know
It ain't nothing that we can do
We ain't got no choice but to let her go
She don't wanna be home no mo
She got her bags packed headed out the do
Do you want to go
No
Hmmm we'll fine I don't wanna go
I wanted you to go, I know, I just didn't want go

#35

The last drink for tonight
Can I have one more
Before they say good night
Okay but don't get in a fight
Seems like trouble finds him every night
It's odd and he ain't even been drinking tonight
I guess he already knows who causes the fight
Uhhh unn good night
Don't talk to me for the rest of the night
Silent is how they treat him
Quite he remains so theres no fuss or fight
Quick to draw on the quick draw
If things collide will it be with a jaw
He got hit with something he never saw
Tit tit !!!tapping on the window of the car
It was her tapping on the window of the car

On another note
We could be on another planet
And I would jam it
Put it on a sandmich
I said with the crust off
When you make my sandwich
Never mind Ill get it
Come on Hand it
I'll make my own sandwich
Got damn it
Don't use the lords name In vien
I stepped on. Lego
And screamed…..
A hand got handed
Over my mouth I could have use it
The shit was like the potty had to use it

#37

underated
Chasing paper
Death only means well See our maker
Grinding in thunderstorm
Girl I can't wait to see you when I get home later
Your gonna have to take a break from your phone tellem you'll talk to
them later
Let's light a blunt
And go to the ozone
Let's get So high we forgot we where home
This homemade got me feeling like I'm not at home
I'm flying so high, flying above my home
I'm waiting until my parents get home
Bss bss
I got n alert nigga I'm grown
Shits and mfs giggles
On the phone A he- he I was just fucking with you nigga

#38

bird watching
Early mornings drinking coffee
Smoking on a blunt
Ive just spotted one
Mockingbirds
Blue jays
Robins
Cardinals
Uwww I see one
Red winged black birds
I forgot the names of the little ones
Elmer fudge this one is a little rascally one
Yeah what's up Doc
Your behind in time
You don't have Tik tok
I know but I still rock

#39

Damn girl your pretty like you just came from heaven
Stay like that don't change
Kinda stubborn resistant to change
I will but I will stay in my lane
Holding stearin wheels
Gripping grain
I went against the grain
So much I got splitters on both hands
Ohhw to hot to touch man
Hot potato hot potatoes
I remember when all
We had to eat was potatoes
Does this go with that
I don't know
Flavins mixing
It was some good times being po

#40

A nigga Marshawn Lynching
A nigga in best mode
All about that action
Lights camera action
A nigga can read the subtitles
Just like he can read the caption
No capping
Graduated gown and cap and
Diploma in Hand
Yeah you know I'm a the man
He told me I couldn't do it
Look at me
No he want to shake my hand
Damn he was wrong about a man
No doubts
I know he can get it done, like me he's a man

#41

She wants pay back
Bzz bzzz
She just hit me back
Where you at
The same spot where you left me at
No hard feelings
You know I don't know where my feelings are at
Next to you in bed
I've laid, kneeled and sat
Took off my shirt and my hat
You know where this ends at
I'm glad you came back
I'm really sorry
It's not even you
It's just some thing that happened way back
Give me a hug I'm glad you got my back

#42

I got your back
I got your back bitch
We besties
And I got yo back bitch
Tell these niggas they better stop
They don't know me bitch
I'm from I'll stab an nigga
I'll stab a bitch
I don't give a damn who they are
I'll cut a bitch
Creases in My jeans and With out me they still standing
Mending wounds I didn't mean to be so demanding
I was being the responsible one for the family
For the choice I made
Now they don't want to call me family
Gotta love them from the distance talking about family

#43

Shout out to my family For getting over addictions and gambling
Breaking generational curses
I'm like moses In these versus
If i hitem too hard the next person their calling are the po po s
the doctors
and the nurses
Call the corners and funeral directors
Begin Lining up their hearses
I'll Knock out all the opponents in any versus
No print or cursive
Greens cornbread and turnips
Even when she's mad shell gives me a kiss
Where has the love been likes this
Behind all the walls built by lies and
Actions speaks louder than words
She sees 's, like damn man slow down, for Jesus Christ and shhhsh

#44

Baby I'm tired
I'm just calling to let you know I'm thinking about you
I'm just working on keeping my cool
Life try's to bulling like the bully's in school
This time i rather not fight you and keep my cool
I still don't know why you want to fight me after school
I like everyone at this school
I think everyone is cool
I know they pick at me to see if I'mma lose my cool
I'm alright, it won't be the the first time staying after school
I dont know man I gotta find my own way home after school
Don't worry about it, my momma said it's okay to give you a ride after
school
So your the little boy my son says He doesn't want to fight at school
What's your problem young man
I don't know, we'll don't worry about it
Let it be the last time it happens at school, headed to get ice cream after
school

#45

Heavenly Father bless me
I know I should have no worries
I'm alive n not in obituaries
Visiting loved ones
I was at the cemetery
It's been awhile since I seen you
I think the last time I saw you was January
Valentine's Day February
Sometimes thinking about death is scary
Getting older broke and weary
God thank you for hearing me
I know things are in the works
I just can't see
Faith I walk blindly stepping
I'm not falling if he's catching
Even when they try to knock me over he sets me up right

#46

Gentlemen
I'll open the door for you
My heart I'll pour out to you
That's what you want
I'll give it to you
I just got eyes for you
Why would I do that to you
Don't worry about I'll get it for you
No you don't owe me nothing
It's all for you
What else could I do
When your gone I get to thinking about you
Would you do those bad things to me
Sometimes I'm scared of you
I love you to death
Still after death I want you

#4

You say your my friend
Why are you talking about my friend
She never said any of those things
I don't even know where this starts or begins
Drama who care it's all pretend
A broken heart is hard to mend
It hurts it can't be pretend
I lost my best friend
Friends to very end
Genuinely I love and miss you my friend
Let me know when we can catch up and have a few drinks my friend
It's been a while since I seen her or him
I know I didn't say that because I don't have nothing to say about to nobody my friend
I wrote a note that said I love everybody in the end
They can see my words
Because if they hear my words the may misconstrued words I don't want them mess up the obituary in the end

#48

Fitted hat
Chains no cap
Hoodie
You look just like that one rapper that raps
Which one is that
Flattery just to get that
Hand out, asking for a dollar
Why not, don't bother
Hard working blue collars
Going to school to be a scholar
Lost his job
Now he don't have a single cent or a dollar
Angry things come out with a holler
Ask him for change, why bother
Be the change that refuses to change
It's a tennis match in my brain, his out an ankle strain

Without you In this world
this place wouldn't be the way it is
I know sometimes we don't see our purpose here, but look there it is
look deeper into it and you'll see it
Look at all the people around you and you'll see it
How can you really say that your alone
When there are people there in that home
Sometimes your just stuck in your head and wrong
Silly rabbit your never alone your just Thinking your alone
Your crowd is out there in a different home
Even if it's just you there your not alone
You can go out side and see natural tones
You see your not alone
They might not be humans but your not alone
And even in nature things get alone
In your body you have millions of cells
So how can you be alone

#50

Man it's hard shit
You come back home and the love of your life don't want to talk shit
I wonder what happened while I was gone away shit
I know what happened at the place where I was at shit
Memories take me back
Bombs drop, people scat
The injured scream for Doc, laying on their back
Men grabbed litters and placed the American causality on their back
Oh the terrible things we heard when we got back
I ain't trying to hear none of that
While rocket propelled grenades where flying she was on her back
Boom!!!..on the ground soldiers fell back
She wonders why he won't talk to her when he got back
In silence or fear, she won't talk about that
He's like you shouldn't have to hide that
He's been through worse than where she's been at

#51

Going out the gate, never knowing if your coming back
Still it's like a dream, Damn!!!, years later like Dog I'm back
Looking for his Dogs, it's nobody but him and his service dog in the back
for him he has to get service dogs to watch his back
Daily life, sight, sounds, and smells have him flashing back
In a room the walls always has his back
Anxieties and panic attacks
Where is the exit located at
Grabbing his forehead, he's tired of the flashbacks
He's like that's not where he planned to be at
I guess she thought he wasn't coming back
She moved on before he had a chance to make it back
Now he's back, you can't find her, what a knife in the back
Back home with orders to go back
Shanking his head like Man!!!, I just got back
Soldiers know Uncle Sam don't give a fuck about that

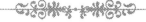

#52

So much mental anguish it's about to collapse
Heated arguments, he gets slapped
Defending himself he strikes back
Some how he ends up with the cuffs behind his back
Is that fair for soldiers, listening to my soldiers getting back
Now he's the leader with the cuffs behind his back
The same things happened to us when we got back
I guess his love didn't do him like that
If she did him like that how would he react
He already said she would get laid out in the back
I guess she never should have put her hands on him looking back
So a man can't protect himself and hit them back
Come on man she's a female
Yeah and she should be in jail
The tragedies of being a male
It's so hard being a male

#53

Haters in the stands
I'mma do a trea young
I'mma hit a game winner
Urt urt I'mma do my little dance
It's silent
crickets in the stands
Six ounces flour
Two ounces sugar
Six ounces butter
I just taught you how make some bread
People thinks she's crazy she's just in her head
talking to herself scenarios play in her head
But shes talking to her children
That are no longer hear but she can see them in her head
When I heard tear's formed in my head
I miss my children and the only place I get to see them is in my head

#54

Emilia Tereza Harper said
Be happy
Be Happily Married and Happily Living,
a cure to illness and how to live in harmony
Listening to wise word
I've been stay away from things that harm me
I won't that love that swarms me
I'll fight for my queen
She's my little bumble bee
Im the sunflowers
She gets the nectar from me
Im just your little sunflower
And your sweet like me
With out the sun you couldn't see
Bzz Bzz that was a kiss from me to you
A kiss that sounded like a little bee given to you

#55

He went to go
But she wouldn't let him go
Let me go
I don't understand why you would tell me to go
Then get mad when i get ready to go
I'm just mad I really don't want you go
Hurtful words said we know how that feels though
If you know that why would you still say it
Shoulders shrug
I don't know
Watch out the way
Let me go outside and think about it though
I'll be back but I think we need to take a break though
I don't understand how you took that as I wanted to separate from you
Hold on baby
Baby I got you

#56

I wanna be that book you read
Early in the morning
I'm right next to clock
when it goes off alarming
I brought the book that you where yearning
I also brought you some coffee,
You know it's gonna be a good morning
The Pages written by me
I just love informing
If your hands get cold you can use the cup for warming
Remember Relax, look at you yawning
She's like I know hes a good man, adoring
She's like babe look a prime example of a man, roaring
Pages turned, not one page is boring
He's like why did you wait to tell me this morning
No fuss or fight she was just mourning

#57

Listening to love sleep
she was snoring
Grieving in the day now it's dawning
Reminiscing in the night, she's glad it's not scorching
Looking out the window it's pouring
She said I'm just Waiting until tomorrow, she was imploring
Evading the horrors of night under the awning
She realized the arrows shot by Cupid was just his love spawning
Love sown so deep they could see the love they wanted forming
Love made under the sheets makes you want to save it like hoarding
Pockets of love can be seen on the flooring
Alarms ring, beep beep now it's morning
Deep slumbers couldn't keep them sleep this morning
Restating facts, well according
She woke up out of nightmares, warring
To aid with the issues, he knew keeping her safe aided positive reinforcing

#58

They Read ever chapter and now they feel like everyday is worth scoring
Doubt, a feeling that's worth exploring
Like I didn't know, what the fuck, exhorting
Is the coffee getting cold I don't mind rewarming
Cat got your tongue ?
no, this just helps with the sorting
Don't feel bad it was just a scorning
The past over but remind yourself to pick up back where you left off this
morning
But whats wrong with transforming
Move out of situations and environments even when it's storming
Smell the coffee, Damn new places feels good like reforming
The Aroma of coffee is the star of this show, and it's performing
French roast coffee is also good, forewarning
Another sip of coffee, and your taste buds will begin absorbing
The Taste of coffee on the tip of tongue is restoring
Listening to what makes his and her heart beat is underscoring and very
rewarding

#59

Thank you for reading me and good morning
P.S reading some books maybe unrewarding
This one is sealed with a kiss, to help with enduring
I hope this help, it's like encouraging
words and hugs that are supporting
Who cares if your separated or divorcing
Smile in court and be a smart husband
Wives attack a man
He a good fellow
Now he's a bad man
Who cares what they tell the judge man
Not one day have they walked in your shoes man
We know it's fabricated don't worry about it man
I bumped into the judge
She was just trying use you man
I was helping you out, I see this all the time man

#60

One more day closer to I achieve what I've been working on
I had it planned
I had to get my hustle on
In my pants a man full grown
I don't now what they do in their home
Waking up prayers straight off the top off dome
Yawn and stretch
Grab my dick
Walk down the hallway and take piss
Take shower, I might have to take a shit
Look in the mirror brush my teeth
And tell my self I got this
A boss tying my tie up
One button when i button up
A lil shoe wax for the shoes that are scuffed up
I love you baby tapping that boot, im late get up

Resting bitch face
What's wrong with you
Looking at your face
Sad about an old altercation
Come on now and let's face
That stuff is no longer in your face
Ain't that great
Your no longer in that place
I know they pop up
Like your reliving that moment in that place
The only way to get over that is to make new memories in place
Mise in place your food is on the plate
I know but the meal reminds me of when I was at that place
I'm sure it does it's not the same meal from that place
But it's doesn't have the same taste
Mmmm mmmm your right this has a great taste

#62

There nothing like kissing your lips in this place
Things are bulging in another place
It's something about kissing your lips
That's put me in the place
Licking different parts in the space
You should see your face
I Can't see you right now there a pillow over face
I didn't put there
All I can hear is moaning
And ecstasy on your face
I can see your lip biting I can see your beautiful face
I can see you grabbing for things all over this place
I love it when you grab me by my ears on my face
Pulling me towards you im about to land another kiss on your face
Do you want me to kiss you in that other place
The waterfalls I like to taste

#63

Reminiscing about high school
She left me a hickey
Got up off of me
And the next day tripped on me
And said who left this hickey
Because it sure wasn't me
Your the only woman I been with
Unless during sex you change up on me
Split personality
A gangster bitch in the streets
A loving woman in the sheets
Don't worry baby there's no other lady
I love you, your very unique
I wouldn't listen to them I would listen to me
They would lead you astray
Hey!!! I'm saying come here baby, when you need to talk come to me

#64

With clarity
You should be able to think clear
If it's cloudy it ain't clear
No need to bring the problems of yesterday or last year
Your focus is on and in the moment
and your thinking has to be clear
Make a decision where you won't regret it in a year
Before you do it
Will it effect you or me in year
I've been so sweet and sincere
I get angry to and sometimes it's hard to think clear
Heart pounding
Tunnels lights
Feeling like Im blacking out
I run to bed the so I don't hurt myself if I fall out
Bad responses, I'm fighting to get out

#65

How would you think of you woke up brand new
Friends are like What happened to you
I don't know I grew
I didn't mean to be a shrew
Piercing like the wind
Ok team, Break this is for the win
Holding up the championship
Yeah boy I knew we where gonna win
All the hard work we put in
Taking pictures
He had a big grin
Congratulations on the win
He's mad coach didn't keep him in
I don't know why he didn't keep you in
Your contribution to the side line Contributed to the win
He's hurt, it's time or you to go in

#66

Just let it be
Just let me
Enjoy this moment
I'm pretty sure it ain't just me
Leave him alone
Just let him him be
Leave her alone
Just let her be
My heart is fluttering like a little bee
On a petal
Just let me be
In the end will see
Looking back
Pictures of you and me
At a quinceanera
Hailey just turned sixteen

#67

I'm trying to stop the violinist
Yeah I'm the finalist
I'm more of a pianist
Chipping away I'm doing some damage to it
Just a little piece left, tap it
To hard you'll damage it
Raw uncut
Like a diamond
Before they cut it
And they polish it
It's so old they should abolish it
An abomination when they try to grip it
Hold it tight or you'll get hit
Recoils or kick backs
Bullets discharged, patients on their back
Medics try to patch up soldiers where they been hit in the back

#68

No need to hide
Unknown feelings inside
I can see what your talking about from this side
You can keep it your pride
I'm ready to ride
I see my loves I wave hi
As I pass by
Come here, no need to cry
I realize
The pain when tears drop from the eye
That really means it hurt inside
Wiping tears away from you eye
It's gonna be alright my lady
We got other fish to fry
I know, that's why I keep asking why
Holding hands looking up at the sky

Coaches yell
Players play
Kids scream
Parents yell
The crowd uproars
The ball soars
Left in suspense
The ball is in the air
It's close
It's almost there
One handed catch
Touchdown
He brought it in
Both feet touched the ground
A victory dance
They won at home, Cheers on holy grounds

#70

Stomachs growl
Whistles blow
Flagrant fouls
Tempers go
Come on man
Get away from me bro
The crowd awaits the first blow
Come on man your costing us the game bro
At the come around slow
Be ready for the ball
If you get fouled we still can win with a free throw
Applauding
Stay in the there you go
He won the game
No need to shoot the extra free throw
Yes we did it we just listened to coach

#71

Silent steps in the grass
With the light
we can shed light on their azz
Snakes slither in the grass
If you look closers
It's a mound
Fire ants in the grass
Running, it's not funny
She almost got stung
Swatting bumble bees in the grass
Fragrant flowers allures nectar cravers
Stay calm its a life saver
Kids walk by at night in the grass
Small talk about class
Did you do your homework
Yeah and …. the conversation got quieter as they passed

#72

The drivers sleep
The passenger lays his hand on her thigh
Waiting for time to pass by
While the wait
People pass by
Team captains yell
One two three
PANTHERS !!! The whole team sounds back
Whistle blow, go to the back
On two on two
The team awaits the snap
Offsides
The coach yells
Move back
Kids sigh in frustration
What they don't know is it's the last lap

#73

Roars of you can't be lazy
Let me wipe my glasses my vision is hazy
Private conversations
I don't know why they hate me
On the chopping block
Looking back
Can my linage get some rest
If you put it in a book a nigga won't find it
That statement was false as that statement
Hey man it gotta be a at better than this
In chaos stuck in a book
Rewriting the pages torn out
All lies and fabricated
It was a whole book
They just tore out some pages
And added statements and pages

#74

You can wave hi
They'll roll by
Then you can experience
A person waving hi
Then the other person is just walking by
Man what's up with that guy
Being nice is easy but hard in my eyes
Genuinely caring sometimes they make hard for my guy
On compass, he ran up to old dude
Hey man, Hi
Hey man your that guy
Omg your that guy
Yeah I was just waving hi
I know how it feels to be the other guy
That's why I speed up and said hi
Keep your head up to the sky

#75

One step in front of the one the other step
Stepping is like going up
Your moving forward
No stairs
Come back here", Don't got there
If they really loved me they would care
Almost at the finish line
He does have a choice but to get there
Because if he loses
He'll have to go back there
Disappointed sitting in there chair
He knows he does belong there
He's gotta dig dip if he's gonna get there
He's gotta dig a Little Deeper to hold the trophy in the air
He's gotta dig a little deeply to pop champagne and squirt it in the air
He's gotta dig a little deeper there's an explosion and smoke in the air

#76

Monster cans
Dirty pants
Lovers dance
Midnight romance
Girl I love you
No need to take off your pants
I don't want a one night stand
I want to be your man
On one knee give me your hand
Girls like you are high in demand
I guess I'm a lucky man
That's ring looks lovely on your hand
The past is over, come on hold my hand
Quite all that talking out your next
Girl I understand, you deserve the best
I'm honestly doing my best

I'mma put you on top
When I get ready call you your on top
I guess they didn't want the championship spot
Their falling back
Now there in the number two spot
And there in the number three spot
Ohh shit look who's in the number one spot
Going over the finish line, hands go over top
I love your kisses, wetter than a mop
I love when you give top
I love when your on top
Your right I'm hitting that spot
Yeah I know I play around a lot
Naked and just socks
I didn't mean to throw you off top
I told you one day I'll be at top

#78

her mind was rough like sea
Some things she said had me jerking
Oh!! Shit !!! That's a big ass wave
I think it's about take us under
She's laughing,
Come on now you want die
Your right I'll quit being a pussy
Just don't push me
Flashbacks looking at his hands
They use to pick on him until he got fed up
Nawh don't run nawh
With his hands up
Now they ducking with their hands up
If someone touches him he blows up
Now they know more stuff
There a perfect match their so tough

#79

I would love to get to know you
But you won't let me get close to you
It's okay I already know enough about you
I'm not good enough for you
I don't make enough money for you
I don't have a place for you and your kids
You wanna hold my past against me
You know he belongs to me
You'll try to use the children against
Shaking my in therapy
I knew it wasn't me
But look at the damage she did to me
I hear you it looks like she did the same to me
Now I can't spend the time and energy
Stay away from me im finally happy
I learned to stay out of people business because they could harm you or me

#80

Sipping coffee I'm glad you thought of me
Responding back
Hey baby
Good morning
I'm glad to hear from you
Sorry I couldn't talk for long
I'm trying to get things done
I was putting them off for so long
Sinking in the sea
I was trying to see where I fit in this sea
At the body of the sea
I'll be the star fish
you'll see by your feet
Because you'll never look up in the stars to see me
Second thoughts
Tell me where to be and I'll be

#81

#thankyouforbeingyou
There you'll find yourself looking
Pictures of you and me
High achievements
Bishop dressed to the T
C.E.Os encouraging you and me
I don't want to act to high because tomorrow I might fall down
Their still pushing through, they lost their kid the other day
I thank you for being you
Pushing through
The world starts screwing you
How when that's not what I was trying to do
Now maybe you can see it's not you
Just the people around you
You can finally take the blame off you
I love that your finally being you

#82

the bird's are chirping
Sounds like my crowd
I know they can get real loud
You better get out the way because they'll plow
Hit you in the jaw
Look directly in their face and say I never saw
Nawh man we don't fuck with the laws
The only thing that protect you is that badge and that gun he saw
Walking by he went for the draw
Oh that's a no no, Kicked off the force
No badge, no gun
Now He's one of them
A criminal and now he don't fuck with laws
Ca caw !!crowing like a crow, there goes the law
The new cop shot in the air
Here we go again at another protest and their chanting "things aren't fair."

#83

Oh how do you say things aren't fair
Holding your hands at the fair
Manured
funnel cake
Lemonade thrown thrown in the air
Shots fired
Now theirs a panic in the air
Looking at the news they just aired
Oh my god !!!we where just there
God works in mysterious ways
Baby I love you, I'm glad we got into that argument and got out of there
Because if we didn't we would still be their
We were sitting right there
I knew something was wrong, drones where in the air
I'm glad we got out of there
The was the last time we went to a fair

#84

At a campfire
Sitting by the flames
Drinking James
Shrugging shoulders
I know damn well their not gonna change
I've changed so much they can't see the change
I'm blue in face like a hundred dollar bill
I'm not a group of bills and some some change
Shaking my head
Why do I always have to break like change
I don't want talk, the phone rang
Beep. I just want to tell you that, I love you and I'm sorry, I know it's been
hard since you got out the army
But I need someone here to hold me
Kiss me and I want you be next to me
Beep
Hello thank you for being their since I got out the Army

#85

He's not my peer
He's not my boss
He makes me think of everything that I lost
Time out, that can't be right
We gonna be crammed tonight
Come on!!! We need to get it together
We don't need to act like that tonight
Yeah your right
When adrenaline kicks in
Your ready to fight
Well you shouldn't have been talking shit the other night
It's hard to calm down when your blood is boiling and your ready to fight
You just have to remove to pot from the stove you'll learn some things in
life
He's still piping hot, he'll cool down, Leave him alone for the night
Lay a towel down and it won't be another fight
Baby all I was trying to say is we have to take care of the things we have
in life

#86

what's up man
You done came along way man
Further than What I can
The Last time we chilled was band
I was 16 am now I'm close to forty man
I wonder why she's worried by my ex
Talking to therapist he answered I don't know man
He chuckles, quit Frankly
I don't even know man
It's good to talk to a level head man
But a level headed woman
Is like being in heaven
Hey what you doing
Alright look at you man
I was just calling to see how you doing
Im doing good but hey when are you gonna let me be your man

#87

Close to my dreams
Just another few steps
almost paid off
Just a few more steps
a few more checks
In my bank account
Off my check list
Urrrt, check
Check out my outfit
I got another check
Met the deadline
Everything done
Another check
It's time the last time I checked
We did it
What's next

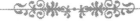

#88

I didn't think he would do it but he did it
Girl I learned my lesson
When he say he gone do it
He gone do it
Shaking her head, Girl, I'm lost in words, I told him he couldn't do it
I hate that I kicked him to the curb because he did it
Did you see him get out that new burb
Girl, that ain't no burb
thats an Escalade
Did you she his dreads, did you see his girl and did you see his smile on his face
Girl he's so handsome I wish I could touch his face but you know i got a bae
That nigga ain't been right since Faye
I talked to him the other day and he said he wasn't worried about Faye
Listening to the man himself it was never him back in the day
Just Faye
Girl He said man if I wouldn't never left I would been sitting at the house fighting with Faye.

#89

ain't nothing wrong with locking the door to make sure your safe
You don't have to give the the code to the safe
You don't have to tell them about the secret place
You don't have to put it in their face
Let 'em hear in the bass
Arff Arff mother fucker get the fuck out my face
I see why hes barking in they face
Because I experienced it myself
Nigga get the fuck out my face
Get out of with all that bullshit
Nigga lifted his shirt and showed his s
The other nigga lifted up his shirt and said me too kid
A nigga almost lost his Łidz to Nigga who lost his lid
Real talk talking about caps and capping watch out for yours kids
And Man please watch out for the kids
They ain't got nothing to do with this

#90

Gotta thank a kid
Thought I did shitty
That's awesome coming from another kid
I wish I could draw that
But I don't see what I did
I couldn't see where he was coming from
He turned it upside down
I was like oh shit kid
Thank you kid
Your so lucky kid
You gotta dad that loves you
You gotta person telling you he doesn't love you
You gotta person trying to get in between you too
There setting themselves up for failure
Nothing can come between you two
Unless you put up barrier's between you

#91

Unn unn the food is done warming
Star-troopers are storming
Just got a call from the foreman
He told me don't worry about coming in
The weather is to bad for us to come in
Put a movie in
Gotta get something to eat I'm starving
Getting paid and I didn't have to come in
That's the greatest thing about working remote
Some days you don't have to go in
At the new job trying to fit in
Guess I don't fit in
In only come in when I have to come in
Cant work with them
He don't won't there works ethnics to rub of him
He'll be pumping iron at his desk getting it in, ain't no excuse for him

#92

She said she loved this song
Woah
Oww
Hand me another beer
I love the part off the song
The crowd whoo hoo'd
They sung along
I love being with you
I wouldn't be here without you
That song wasn't about God in an interview
It was about my wife,
it was a song that i dedicated to her for helping me in life
Say Mane, I love my wife
Without her I can't sleep at night
I worry about my wife
Aww you couldn't sleep either the other night

#93

Ain't seen you since ninety two
On two different paths
Who ain't had misfortune too
Guided the wrong way
Who ain't bounce back yet and who ain't recovered too
Boy yeah you right
So that means that happen to you when you where two
Daddy was doing his best, he wasn't trying to leave you
People weren't doing what they where supposed to do
It was all On him and then she took off with you
So you see it wasn't your daddy's fault or you
If you go look at the photos and the videos in her phone and the papers
in your moms vault
you'll know it wasn't yours daddy's fault
She won't never say it her fault
Shell always make it daddy's or someone else fault
He was doing what he was supposed to do, you gotta watch out for what
comes outta momma's mouth, he already knows you'll figure it out, I just
sat back and figured out

#94

Umm Umm
Your beautiful the way you are
I can't call it
How was your day
It was good and yours
My day is alright
I had to take some time to sit back and write
Reflect back on life
Snap out of it
And get back to life
I'm happy at the spot where I'm in life
I thought I wouldn't have been further
But I'm close to home in life
Thought I would've have been further away in life
If you go up the freeway and make a right
Go down the road make a left and make another right you'll see me on the left on the right

#95

Sitting by the window
Pulling down the visor
Hand me my shade s
Pulling off in the Nissan
Headed out town to see my favorite auntie and my favorite cousin Shawn
We just got back from Guam
Out in the country like bees family swarm
Where we're at was warm
It never got cold, my step mom kept the ac on
No rap music, just church music on
Man who made this song
Kinda sounds like my life
But that ain't all that goes on
Reflecting back on life and we all had something going on
Yeah I know that was years ago I'm sorry and can we move own
R I P to my kids, I got there names tattooed on my arm

I know God got blessings coming our way
I don't know all what really happened the other day
I know it was the past, I know it comes to mind day to dAy
Honestly I just began to pray
Just once @night
I prayed during the day
I prayed at lunch
I'm up to three times a day
It's hard dealing with faith
Walking blindly I'm continuing stepping out on faith
I don't care what they say
That's not my fate
They would love me to miss the time and the date
The when and where
But I remember why and how I'm in this place
I'm the drummer drummer marching in place you should see their face...
boom ah boom boom tit

#97

I got to thank you
Because it was nobody but you
I was trying to get a hold of you
I'm sorry for the things that you had to go through
Some things where unnecessary
When they hazed you it was scary
I wonder why they where yelling like they where in the military
Damn that happened in October And now past February
Yeah she said shes be dealing with it January
November yeah not not January
I gotta take it so it can rejogg my memories
Yeah that happened to me but I ain't gone let that bother me
It's seems like the boogey man but there playing tricks on you and me
Theses feelings and emotions that we got between you me
Listening Tupac pass me that Hennessy
Sipping on an ice cube God murder my enemies and burn at a thousand degrees

#*98*

Down on my knees I fall
I wanna quit
But I cant give up y'all
I'm so tired but im gonna come get y'all
I told you I'll be there when you call
I'm upset that you didn't call
You don't have to be ashamed because sometimes we fall
We're Gonna be alright
We made it through another day
We made it through another night
We're gonna make it through this
That ideas perfect
I just want you know it will be worth it
Don't give up and work through it
It's worth keeping don't toss it
Your gonna be madder if you get some new shhh

Let me tell you girl
He loves you
Your the center of his world
You and him
Plus your kids and his kids
That's his world
Sister Don't blow it all gambling in this world
He put it back, loving his girl
I know if I do this I'll lose my girl
Baby you don't need to gamble
Your his world
Without you he doesn't have a world
He's not worried about another girl
He's focused on you girl
He loves you girl
I see what he sees in you, your a great woman, girl

#100

I hope you got to see things my way
Ain't nothing like cruising with you on the highway
Uhhh I'm riding with my baby
Got the top down on the freeway
We had to go around the back way
I was so happy she took my hand and looked my way
Can I get a kiss from my baby
Land one right there baby
A man ain't crazy for wanting affection and love from his baby
Hold my hand baby
I love you lady
When I don't get your love I go crazy
me too baby
Are You gonna stop by see me
You know I am baby
See later I gotta go work baby

Printed in the United States
by Baker & Taylor Publisher Services